THE MANY DUMB THINGS THAT I DID IN MY LIFETIME, FOR YOUR READING PLEASURE

By Jack L. McSherry, Jr.

December 2019

EATING DIRT FOR GOOD HEALTH

When I was about four years old, I took a break from my outdoor activities and went in the house where my mother was entertaining a visiting lady.

I was in an adjacent room, but I could hear them discussing various things. Apparently they were discussing children and their unsanitary habits. The visiting friend thought that the bad habits were not too serious because I heard her make the statement to my mother that kids probably should eat a certain amount of dirt just to remain healthy. I'm sure she was just joshing.

However, hearing that, I immediately went outside, scooped up a handful of dirt from our unpaved driveway and ate it.

THE DESK SCRATCHING EPISODE IN THE FIRST GRADE

When I started school, I was five years old, in the first grade, in the local elementary school. My teacher was a very nice lady. Her name was Jemima Eltringham. While Miss Eltringham was discussing items of learning with the students, I was sitting at my desk, near the back of the room. I was not listening to what she was saying and was bored with the proceedings. For some unknown reason, I proceeded to chew the eraser off of my wooden pencil and exposed the all-metal enclosure of the eraser. Since the first grade was located within a fairly recent new addition to the school, the chairs and desks were brand new. I placed the metal end of the pencil onto the top of the wooden desk and proceeded to rotate it on the surface of the desk. I diligently continued this procedure until the entire top of the desk was adorned with curving and looped scratches.

Apparently Miss Eltringham noticed that I was doing something that was not in accordance with the normal procedures of learning. She approached my desk and noticed the modified surface of the desk. She immediately went into some form of extreme excitement and left the classroom to locate the principal of the school who was a lady named Dorothy Pensyl. After a few minutes, Miss Eltringham returned to the classroom with Miss Pensyl in tow. They stood behind me as I sat in my seat at the desk and excitedly talked about the modified surface of the desk. One of them produced a cloth and some kind of liquid which she used to wipe the entire surface of the desk. As I watched the proceedings, while sitting at the desk, I concluded that the wiped surface looked much better. However, the two ladies obviously did not think the surface of the desk looked good. They required that I stand up alongside the desk, and they produced some brown rope from somewhere, which they used to tie my hands together behind my back. I was then marched to the front of the room, and to the corner of the room. Then I was instructed to stand in the corner, facing the corner. The two ladies left me there and went back to their work. However, I refused to face the corner, and instead, turned around and faced the class with a very indignant look on my face. Commands to me to face the corner had no effect so I spent the entire afternoon standing in the corner glaring at the class. Since the rope around my hands was not tied very tightly, I slipped my one hand out of the binding and stood there with one hand free and the other hand having a rope hanging from it. The teacher did not try to change that situation, she just ignored me and allowed me to spend the remainder of the class day standing in that corner. I happened to be wearing my high-top shoes at the time. This style of shoe had a leather pocket in it in which a pocket knife was stored. The kids in the class thought that I leaned down, took the pocket knife out of the pocket of the shoe, and cut the rope to get loose. That was not true, but I allowed the class to believe it.

Jack, age 5, in 1933

PANTLEG ON FIRE, I RAN INTO THE HOUSE FOR HELP.

In the early 1930's, when I was about six years old, we lived in Sunnyside. In our back yard, there was an area of no grass and no vegetation. That is where Dad would burn our trash. This one day, I was in the back yard and went to the burn site. It appeared that there was no fire there at the time, so I walked into the ashes and started kicking a tin can around. After a little time, I looked down and the right pantleg of my overalls was on fire. I panicked and ran about a hundred feet, and into the kitchen where I found my Mother. When she saw me standing there with my pantleg burning, she knelt down alongside me and beat the fire out with her hands.

I don't remember being scolded or warned about doing things like that, but I probably was. However, as soon as the fire was put out, I went back outside and who knows what brilliant thing I would do next.

BONES AND POISON IVY

At the age of seven, I was walking around in the fields adjacent to my home, which was a common pastime of mine. These fields were unusual because they were never farmed or put into any obvious use. The owner of the land never had any problems with anyone walking in these fields. Several fields were delineated by brush rows, growing wild, between the fields. These brush rows contained underbrush and trees.

On this particular day, as I was walking past one of these brush rows, I noticed some bones laying on the ground surrounded by underbrush. I crawled into the underbrush to get a better look at the bones. There were many bones, unattached, but interesting to me because they had unusual shapes. I did not know it at that time, but the bones were actually the backbone of some animal.

I gathered the bones with my hands and placed as many as I could into my pockets, and carried the remainder in my hands. I took them home and showed them to my mother. She was not totally happy with my find, but she allowed me to keep them. I took them out into our back yard and laid them in the grass. After I examined them, and when my excitement eventually subdued, I moved onto other activities.

The next morning, when I wakened from a night's sleep, I got out of bed, but I had a problem opening my eyes. My face, and my entire body was swollen and itchy. When my mother observed me, she was quite concerned. She thought that I may have contracted some strange disease because of my handling of those old bones.

She called our family doctor whose practice was in the town of Shamokin, which was located about three miles from our home. Doctors made house calls at that time, so Doctor Harris came to our house to check me out. After talking to me and after examining me, Doctor Harris concluded that I was covered with poison ivy.

The doctor gave me a bottle of rubbing alcohol to put on the poison. He told me to stay out of the sun, and be as inactive as possible.

Over the next few days, I developed fluid filled blisters on my legs, and extreme poison ivy on all parts of my body.

Apparently when I crawled into the underbrush to gather my treasure of bones, the underbrush was a heavy growth of poison ivy.

For the next several weeks, I itched with poison ivy. I was quite uncomfortable, however, I did not stay in the house. I still found things to do around the house, and I also wandered around the neighborhood and did things with my friends.

When the big blisters on my legs itched, I scratched them vigorously with the sides of the soles of my shoes. Of course this broke the blisters and probably spread the poison on my legs.

To minimize the spreading of the poison, the Doctor told me to stay out of the sun, however, when I sat in a sunny area, the heat made the itching areas feel much better, so I spent a lot of time sitting in the sun.

Eventually, after several weeks, the poison ivy gradually diminished and eventually went away. I was back to normal.

I was very happy to be rid of the poison, and I am sure that my Mother was also relieved.

But, would you believe it, later, in several weeks, I once again contracted poison ivy. Apparently I had crawled into another batch of poison ivy. The poison was not quite as intensive as the first batch, but again I was covered with poison ivy. I knew what to do, so I suffered through another uncomfortable bout. I am not sure what my mother was thinking, but she still tolerated me.

FIRE CRACKERS ON THE 4TH OF JULY

When I was eight years old, we liked to celebrate the holiday by setting off fire crackers. Of course, we started this ritual about a week before the holiday and continued it until the day of the holiday. Our source of firecrackers was to purchase them at a local store which was located close to our house. As kids, we had no money, so we would manage to obtain money from our father, as necessary, to proceed with our program.

Our preferred firecracker was about two inches long and about ¼ inch in diameter. They were pretty powerful and made a loud bang. We liked to put them under piles of dirt, or under a tin can so we could watch the splattering results of the explosion. The way to ignite the firecracker fuse was with punk. Punk could be purchased in the store, but we preferred to get our punk in the nearby woods. It was free that way. The punk was a dried piece of fungus that grew on the sides of old stumps. One piece of punk could be lighted with a match and would maintain the hot spot all day.

So this one evening, after dark, we kids were lighting our firecrackers while holding them in our hand, then throwing them out in front of ourselves to explode. However, on one occasion, I lighted my firecracker fuse, but was busy talking to someone so I forgot to throw my firecracker away. It exploded in my hand. This incident numbed several of my fingers and my thumb for several hours thereafter.

The next day, we were again playing with our firecrackers. At one point, my brother, Bill, and his friend John Cook, were pushing firecrackers into the spaces between boards in the siding of my Dad's garage, then ran back to watch them explode. The fuse on one of these firecrackers burned to within a quarter inch of the firecracker, then went out. In a discussion between the two of them, neither one wanted to relight that fuse. I told them that I would light it. I had a plan. The firecracker was located about two feet from a corner of the garage. I told Bill and John that I will stay around the corner of the garage, then reach around the corner and light the short fuse. I would be safe that way. So I reached around the corner to light the fuse, but I could not see it so I had trouble lighting it. Therefore, I looked around the corner as I lit the fuse. The firecracker exploded instantly as soon as I lighted it and fire and debris flew from it. It burned a hole in my cheek about an inch below my right eye. First aid for the hole was to go into the house and wash that area of my face, the remainder of the healing was left to Mother Nature.

Jack, 8 years old

GOING FOR A BIKE RIDE

When I was about eleven years old, on a nice sunny day in the summertime, I went for a bicycle ride with a friend, Wayne Taylor. Wayne met me at my house in Sunnyside, then we rode our bikes to the nearby village of Overlook. As we arrived in Overlook, we decided to take a ride on Airport road, a dirt road that had no name at that time. From where we started, the road was mostly down hill for quite a distance, so we rode easily ahead on that road. After we travelled a short distance, wayne said, "lets race." So we both pedaled faster and were each picking up speed. Wayne was out in front of me as we were both travelling at top speed. This being a dirt road meant that at times of heavy rain it would get muddy, and when it became muddy, the wheels of the cars would sink into the mud thereby making deep ruts in the road. When the road dried, the ruts would solidify into hard ruts. As I was pedaling at top speed, about 50 feet behind Wayne, and going down a slight hill, my front wheel dropped into one of those ruts, whereby the front wheel collapsed and I flew over the handlebars and landed violently on my stomach onto the road. Apparently as I was doing this, there were two farmers standing at their house a short distance from the road and they witnessed the occasion. When I woke up, these two farmers were standing alongside me and looking down at me as I lay on the road. The one said, " I thought I would find you dead". Wayne Taylor did not know that I had a problem and he kept going. After a short time, he noticed that I was not following him, so he turned around to locate me. I guess the farmers concluded that I was not going to die, so they went back about their business while Wayne and I pondered our trip back home. It was about a mile and a half trip back home. So I lifted up the front of my bike, because the wheel was totally twisted out of shape, and headed for home. Wayne walked, and sometimes rode his bike, and accompanied me back to my house. As we approached the house, my Dad was standing there watching my arrival with the bike with the twisted wheel. His welcoming comment was simply, " what did you do this time?" After a few days, my Dad had my bike repaired and I was ready for more adventures.

Jack, 11 years old

I TRIED TO SCARE SOME HUNTERS IN THE ADJACENT FIELD

Several other kids and myself were staying in my Uncle's cottage for the weekend. I was about eleven years old at the time. The cottage was situated in the woods alongside a creek, and separated from the adjacent road by a very wide field. It was hunting season for rabbits and pheasants and I spotted several hunters in the field in front of the cottage sneaking through the weeds carrying their shotguns. I liked the rabbits and pheasants and I did not want anyone to shoot them. So I came up with a good idea to get rid of the hunters.

In the living room of the cottage, my uncle had a bear rug, complete with a head and snarling mouth. I picked up the rug and draped it over my shoulders, and put the head of the bear on top of my head. Then I went outside, walked over to a large tree adjacent to the field. I looked around the tree with my bear head and growled at the hunters to scare them away. Either they didn't hear me, or they were ignoring me, because they did not get scared nor did they run away. Perhaps that was a good thing. Maybe if I would have scared them, they would have shot me.

PLAYING WITH EXPLOSIVES

Well, they weren't really explosives, but they were a lot like explosives. When I was about ten years old, my uncle gave a 22 Rifle to my two brothers and me. We had joint ownership of it. However, he did teach us how to use it. He also taught us all of the safety precautions that were required.

However, when I was twelve years old, I found another way to use the rifle. When I shot the rifle, I saved all of the empty cartridges. Then one day I took these empty cartridges and put the head of a strike anywhere match into the empty cartridge, broke off the remainder of the match, then crimped the end of the cartridge to totally seal it off. Then I took my cartridges into the back yard and sat down alongside a paved walkway. I placed one of the cartridges on the walkway, then hit it with a hammer. When it was hit with the hammer, it exploded with a very loud bang.

I enjoyed making the explosions by continuing to hit cartridges with the hammer. Then it happened! When I hit this one cartridge, it exploded and a small portion of the copper cartridge flew from the explosion, went through my overall pants, and penetrated into my leg.

I, somehow, pulled the copper out of my leg, but I had a bloody hole in my leg. Over time the leg healed with the help of Mother Nature. I never told anyone what happened. To this day, I have a white scar on my right leg just above the knee as a remembrance of that brilliant performance

GETTING SMACKED ON THE HEAD AT A RAILROAD CROSSING

When I was twelve years old, we moved from Sunnyside to Tharptown. The distance between the two villages was about two miles. I objected to this move rather loudly, but my parents chose to move anyway. I would now go to a different school than all of my friends. However, I solved that problem by riding my bike or hiking to Sunnyside almost every day, and during school months, every evening.

My parents still owned the house at Sunnyside, so we would occasionally go there to play in our old haunts. This one evening, my brothers, Bill and Dave went to Sunnyside on their bikes, picking up several friends along the way, and they went to our old house. I did not leave home at the same time as they did, but followed a little later to go to the same place to join in on the activities. About half way to my destination, I passed through the village of Weigh Scales. At Weigh Scales, the route to our old house was on a road that left the main highway onto another road that went into Sunnyside. At that location there was a railroad crossing. There was a watchman stationed there at all times to lower the crossing gates across the roadway when a train was appoaching. As I approached the crossing, I noticed a railroad work crew doing some repairs to the tracks a short distance up the tracks. Fascinated with this, I kept an eye on them as I approached the crossing. I did not notice that the gates were down for traffic crossing the tracks, so as I rode, full speed, onto the tracks, my forehead smacked the gate and I was knocked off of the bike. When I woke up, the railroad work crew was standing around me and looking down at me. One of them was trying to talk to me to determine my condition. I concluded that I was ok, so they accepted that and went back to work. I then mounted my bike and proceeded to head for Sunnyside. However, I had a large swollen lump on my forehead and was quite dizzy. I made it to our old house and joined the group. I did not tell any of them what happened. However, that entire evening, I was dazed and just made believe all was well. When the group broke up, we all rode back home. The lump on my forehead went down after a few days and I regained most of my senses. I never told my parents or brothers or anyone else about my episode. Looking back on it, I probably had a pretty intensive concussion.

A TRIP TO PHILADELPHIA

In the year 1941, I graduated from the 8th grade in the elementary school in Tharptown. The school provided us with a trip to Philadelphia. We travelled from Shamokin to Philadelphia on the Reading Railroad. I don't remember most of what we did on that trip, however I do remember, very clearly one thing that I did do.

We were riding on a double decker bus in Philadelhia in the downtown area. I was sitting on the right side of the bus on the upper level. The driver was parking the bus parallel to the curb. As he was backing into position against the curb, I had my window open and was cheerfully watching the people down below on the sidewalk. I stuck my head way out of the bus to get a good look below. As I did this, a man on the sidewalk below yelled at me to pull my head back in the bus. Fortunately, I listened to him and pulled my head back into the bus. Just as I did, the bus was backing into place and there was a metal post there, right on the curb line. It passed the bus within inches and, if I had kept my head out of the window, the post would have sheared my head off.

I almost did not include this dumb event in this book because it is a very scary thought. I don't know who that man was that hollered at me, but I would like to thank him. He kept me alive so that I could do many other dumb things throughout my lifetime.

SWINGING IN THE TREES

At the age of thirteen, I rode my bicycle to an area near our house that was quiet, natural, and contained an irregular landscape with hills, ditches and trees. I rode my bike around in the area, up and down the hills and between the trees. Then I parked the bike and was walking around in the area when I ended up standing at the top of a steeply sloped bank which sloped downward for about fifteen feet. There was a tree growing from the bottom of the slope. There was a horizontal limb, about two inches in diameter, protruding to the right from the tree. Since I did a lot of tree climbing in my lifetime, I decided to jump from the top of the bank to the limb and grab it. Once in the tree, I would climb down the tree to the ground below. However, as soon as I landed on the limb and had a good hold on it, the limb broke off and I landed on the ground fifteen feet below. I didn't break my arms or legs or anything else, so I got back up and looked at the tree in complete puzzlement. In all of my tree climbing, 3/4" diameter limbs always held my weight. Why did this two-inch diameter limb break? I learned something. I usually climbed maple trees, oak trees, cherry trees, and other strong trees. I found out that the tree that broke under my weight was a poplar tree, and it so happens that a poplar tree is one of the weakest and most brittle of all trees. I check the species of a tree before I leap from tree to tree any more.

ICE SKATING WITH MY BROTHER, DAVE.

When I was fourteen years old, in the wintertime, and while living in Tharptown, my brother Dave and I decided to go ice skating on a dam nearby. We walked about a half mile to the dam, put on our skates and began skating around the dam. We were the only ones there, so we had the entire place to ourselves. As we were standing at the one end of the dam, we saw something blue laying on the ice at the other end of the dam. Dave said " I'll race you to that blue thing". So, we both took off at top speed toward the other end of the dam. I got there slightly ahead of Dave, so as I was passing the blue thing, I leaned over to pick it up, to prove to Dave that I was there first. When I leaned over to pick up the object, my feet flew up in the air and my head slammed onto the ice. I instantly had a rather large flow of blood from the right side of my head.

We decided to stop our ice skating fun and hiked home. I washed the blood off of my head and face and it eventually stopped bleeding. Mom never knew that it happened. Mother Nature healed the wounds.

DURING WORLD WAR TWO,

I CONTRIBUTED MY TALENTS TO THE SERVICE OF MY COUNTRY

On my 17th birthday, I enlisted in the United States Navy and served in the Navy for four years.

While in boot camp, we went through many different procedures as directed by our commanding officer. On this one hot morning, the temperature was a little over 100 degrees. We were sent to the drill field, formed ranks, put our rifles on our shoulders, and at the command, began marching throughout the drill field.

We marched all day, taking occasional breaks as provided by our lead marcher. As we were marching, I began to feel hotter in the head than usual, and I also seemed to be getting a sore throat. I said nothing about it to anyone. I just kept marching. Late in the day, just a little before 5:00, we marched to the supply house where we returned our rifles, then we were set free to hike back to our barracks.

When I arrived in the barracks, I went to my bunk and took off my jumper and my tee shirt in preparation to taking a shower. The man in the bunk next to mine looked at me and noticed that my chest was bright red. He then told me that I had scarlet fever and suggested that I go to the sick bay and have it checked out. I , therefore, left the barracks and walked over to the sick bay. The Doctor checked me out and told me that I had scarlet fever. I was then taken to the base hospital and assigned to a bed.

The doctor at the hospital was a crotchety, old gentleman, but he told me that he would give me a double shot of penicillin which would knock the scarlet fever right out of me. Penicillin was a new medicine at the time. He bent me over a desk and gave me the double dose in the seat.

As he promised, in three days, the scarlet fever was gone and I was returned to my boot company.

TRANSFERRED TO THE NAVY BASE AT NEWPORT RHODE ISLAND

After completing my basic training in boot camp, and after graduating from Quartermaster school, I was sent to the Newport Naval base in Rhode Island to await assignment to a ship. While there, I was quarterd in a quonset hut. Transients were assigned to various duties just to keep them busy while they were there. This one evening, I was assigned to stand watch in an unihabited area of quonset huts starting at 11:45 PM until 3:45 AM. I arrived at the site at the proper time of 11:45 PM and met the man who was presently on duty there. He handed me the rifle and I took over. I walked around the desolate area for four hours with the rifle on my shoulder, never seeing anyone during that time period. It was now time for my relief to arrive and take over the watch. However, another hour went by and no one showed up. At about 5:15, no one came to relieve me, so I concluded that I had been there long enough. So I leaned my rifle against one of the quonset huts, walked back to my quarters in a quonset hut, layed in my bunk and went to sleep. Because, I stood the midnight watch, I was allowed to sleep until noon, which I did. I was never questioned about the situation or the abandoned rifle.

Jack, 1945

THE USS HOUSTON

The first ship that I served on was the USS Houston. We were cruising around in the North Atlantic Ocean. The war was over, but we were still looking for hostile German submarines.

After that , I served for about two years aboard the USS Huntington, a light cruiser. I was rated as a Quartermaster 3rd Class. My job on the ship was to stand watch in the pilot house when we were at sea, to write the data for the ship's log, to assist The Navigator to determine our position at sea, and I steered the ship when it was deemed necessay.

This was during the Cold War when we were at odds with the Soviet Union. We toured all over the Mediterranean Sea and visited many foreign ports.

On August 8, 1946, we moored to the dock in Trieste. At the time, Trieste was a free city, but both Italy and Yugoslavia claimed it as theirs. There were constant riots and fighting in the streets between the Italians and the Yuogoslavs. The border between Italy and Yugslavia was called the Morgan Line.

I HIKED INTO YUGOSLAVIA

When we first arrived in Trieste, the entire crew of the Huntington was called together to receive instructions for behavior and activities while in Trieste. One of those instructions was that we were not to cross the Morgan Line. The Morgan Line was the border between Italy and Yugoslavia.

Wherever the ship went, when I went ashore, either alone or with a friend, I would walk throughout the City to observe everything that I thought was interesting. On this one Sunday, I hiked out into the countryside around Trieste. I followed an old dirt road for a long distance then meandered into a field and just kept walking and looking. I suddenly realized that I must have crossed the Morgan Line because I was in Yugoslavia. Of course I was not supposed to have done that, so I backtracked and walked across a field until I was sure that I was back in Italy. I never told anyone that I had been in yugoslavia.

About forty years later, My son, Jack III, was watching a historical program on the television when he called me to come and watch because they were talking about the 1946 problems in Trieste. The Narrator, among other things, mentioned that they are just now clearing the mines from the Morgan Line. I was flabbergasted. They told us not to cross the Morgan Line, but they did not say why. I walked through a live minefield, two ways, and never knew it! They tell me that in the military, you are supposed to do as you are told and don't question why.

ATTACKED BY BANDITS !

On November 23, 1946, the USS Huntington arrived in Alexandria, Egypt and tied up to the dock. The instructions that we received from the command of the ship, to go down town to the center of Alexandria, we should travel by taxi. However, if we chose to walk through the Arab district, we should walk in groups of five or more.

Two of us left the ship and decided to walk through the Arab area of the city to go to the downtown area. We concluded that we did not need a group of five. As we were walking through tbe Arab Area, I noticed a little old man sitting on the sidewalk, but I thought that he was just part of the scenery. However, a short time after, I felt something hit the bottom of the leg of my uniform. I looked down and found that I was hit by some eggs. Immediately, the little old man jumped up, and with a rag, he wiped the eggs from my pantleg. I appreciated what he did and I was about to give him some Egyptian coins. However, he stood up and demanded a tip in American money. Then he pulled a long, curved knife from somewhere and placed it against my ribs. At that point, he told me to give him all of my money. Instantly, my strategy was to punch him in the face and send him flying. After all, he was only a little old man. However, I looked around and saw that we were completely surrounded by very mean looking Arabs, I had to come up with an alternate plan.

We were lucky, because, at that moment, an Egyptian, wearing a black suit and a red fez rode into the crowd on his black carriage pulled by a big, black horse. He told us to jump aboard the carriage, which we did instantly. He then drove us into the downtown area.

Upon arriving in the downtown area, as we went to leave the carriage, he asked us for an exhorbitant amount of money for the ride. I appreciated that he rescued us, but I thought that he was asking for too much. During our little debate, I noticed a policeman standing nearby, so I asked him to intervene. He simply told us to give the man what he is asking for. I gave the driver more than I thought that I should, then we jumped from the carriage and proceeded to observe the sights in the downtown area.

Looking back on it, I believe the whole thing was a concocked procedure for robbing people, and it included the little old man, the circle of mean Arabs, the carriage driver, and the policeman

Maybe we should have walked in a group of five, or possibly taken a taxi.

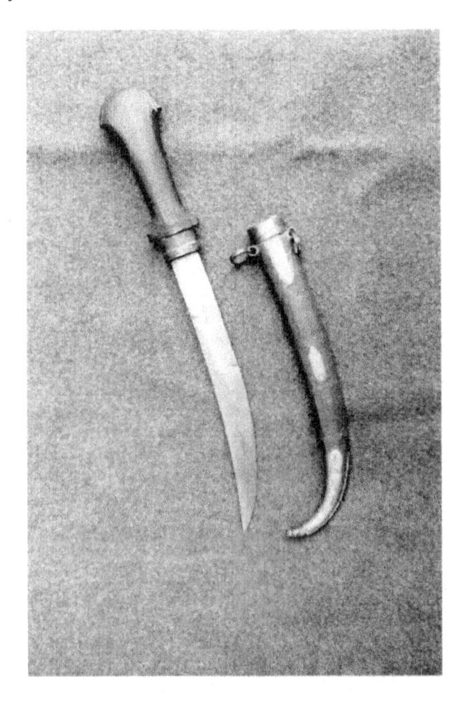

This is the type knife that most Arabs carried.

A FEROCIOUS STORM WITH A BLACK SKY AND THIRTY FOOT WAVES

In 1947, as the Huntington was returning to th United States from the Mediterranean Sea, the ship encountered a strong storm. The sky was black, it was raining, and the ship was rolling at an angle of 39 degrees from the vertical.

The only food that the cooks prepared were sandwiches which could be handled as the ship rolled. As did most of the crew, late in the evening, I went to my bunk. I had to get up for the midnight to 4:00 AM quartermaster' s watch on the bridge.

I woke up a little before 11:30 so I got out of my bunk and headed for the bridge. The storm was still going full blast. I had to be on the bridge 15 minutes before midnight, so I had a little time to spare. I was fascinated by the storm. The sky was very dark, the waves were thirty feet high, and the ship was still rolling at 39 degrees. I decided to walk out on the main deck to get a better view. As I walked out on the deck, it was amazing to look up at those big waves, and to try to maintain my balance on the rolling ship. Suddenly, I heard a loud crash from the bow of the ship. This told me that a big wave broke across the bow, and the main deck would be flooded with water. I did not want to get wet, so I immediately ran across the deck to go through a hatch to get inside. However, I only made it half way across the deck when I was inundated with water up to my chest. At the same time the ship was rolling. The water carried me with it, and to more complicate the problem, with the roll of the ship, the deck that I was on, was sloping toward the sea. I had no choice, I was being shoved toward the side of the ship. As I reached the side of the ship and was being washed overboard, I grabbed a cable in the railing along the side of the ship. I hung onto the cable and pulled myself back onto the deck. Before the ship rolled any more, I quickly ran to the hatch and got inside.

It was now time for me to go on watch on the bridge. When I walked into the pilot house, someone said, "you're soaking wet." I roared back, "no, I am not." There was no further mention of it. I never told anyone on the ship about my experience.

TAKING A HIKE INTO CUBA

After leaving the Mediterranean, once again, on the USS Huntington, we went to Guantanamo Bay, Cuba arriving there on March 1, 1947. Going on liberty onto the Guantanamo Bay Navy base was not very exciting. I was there before and walked all over the base several times. In my wandering on the base this time, I chose to take a hike along the shore line. After walking some distance along the shore, I headed inland. I kept going into the desert- like area. There were no buildings or population, just desert. Then I came upon a little church. It was totally abandoned, but there was a small, fenced-in cemetery alongside the church. Looking it over, I spotted a tombstone marked Frank McSherry who apparently died in the 1700's. I guess he was probably a distant relative of mine.

I continued my hike and was heading further into Cuba. Of couse, we were not supposed to leave the navy Base, and we certainly were not supposed to go into Cuba. However, I found the area to be different and interesting, so I continued my hike. I hiked about five miles into Cuba and the terrain was still the same, unpopulated desert. So I decided to head back to the Navy base. When

I got to within 200 feet of the Base, I was confronted by a rifle carrying Marine. He loudly asked me what I was doing out here. I was on the wrong side of the border between the Base and Cuba. I innocently responded, Oh did I cross the line? The marine yelled at me, yes you are on the wrong side of the line, get back into the base where you belong. I walked across the line and all was well. I did not tell the marine that I was just returning from a five-mile hike into Cuba.

AVOIDING A COLLISION WITH A WHALE IN THE MEDITERRANEAN

USS Huntington

As we were cruising eastward in the Mediterranean Sea in the early evening of a summer day in 1947, I was in the pilot house on duty as the Quartermaster of the watch. The sea was calm, and the water was bright blue. I looked out through a porthole in the pilot house and spotted a whale swimming along on the surface of the water. He was blowing water out of his spout, and just gliding slowly through the water. As I watched, I began to realize that the ship was on a collision course with the whale. I said nothing, but I continued to watch. The officer of the deck in charge of the movement of the ship was on the open bridge directly above the pilot house. There were other people up there also, so I assumed that the officer of the deck would take the necssary action to avoid the whale. Time passed and we were getting closer to the whale. Finally we were getting too close and the officer of the deck was doing nothing. When we reached a point of imminent danger, I threw the levers for control of the two engines of the ship into full speed reverse, and I turned the ship's wheel to make a 90 degree turn to the left. The ship qivered and shook violently. Everyone on the ship could notice that something was happening. I did not have the authority to take that action, but I did not want to kill the whale, nor did I want the ship to be damaged. We did not hit the whale and we returned to our previous speed and direction.

The amazing thing about that event was that I was neither complimented or condemned for taking this action without having the legal authority to do so. As a matter of fact, I never heard anything about it. My theory is that the Officer of the deck possibly explained the action to the captain, called it an emergency, and took full responsibilty, or credit, for the action.

JACK 1947

PAINTING THE SHIP

Periodically, the executive officer would present an order to the crew to paint the ship. Every division on the ship had a space that they worked in, and they were responsible for the cleaning and maintenance of that portion of the ship. With the painting order by the executive officer, each division had the responsibility to paint their area on the ship.

As a Quartermaster, my work space was the bridge, which included the pilot house, the chart house and the open bridge. All personnel in the division participated in the painting of the area.

I did my share of painting the areas within my work space. On this one occasion, I looked up at the foremast, which was within our area of work, and noticed that the metal shield behind the running light on the mast appeared to be in the need of paint. The purpose of this shield was to allow the light to be seen only from the front and to certain angles to the side. I, therefore, acquired my bucket of paint, and a paint brush, and proceeded to climb the ladder rungs that were attached to the side of the mast. Climbing the mast on these projecting rungs while holding a paint bucket and a brush was rather tedious. In additon, the light shield that I decided to paint was about 120 feet above the waterline. I successfully climbed the mast, painted the shield, and returned to the deck below without spilling any paint and without falling to the deck below. No one ordered me to do this task. I took it upon myself to do it. As a result, the procedure meets the title of stupid things that I did and qualifies to be included in this publication.

DETAILED TO SHORE PATROL DUTY IN ORAN, ALGERIA

On June 14, 1947, I was assigned to go on shore patrol duty in the City of Oran. Those who are appointed to shore patrol duty are delegated to go into the city, patrol the streets and bars to keep law and order among the United States Navy sailors, and to have them present themselves to the natives as dignified gentlemen. If any of the sailors did not comply, the shore patrolman had the authority to place them under arrest.

I arrived in Oran at 8:00 in the morning, armed with a 24" long club. I began my patrol, and after a short time was joined by a shore-patrolman from the French Navy. We walked side-by-side along the streets of Oran, but we could not talk to each other because he could not speak English and I could not speak French. However, we did communicate just enough to get along by using sign language.

The Frenchmen and I did not encounter any unruly actions by either French or American sailors, so we just enjoyed our hiking and admired the scenery. At noon, by sign language, the Frenchman let me know that he was going to leave me to go to meet his relief who will take over his duties. That got me to thinking, I should also be relieved after four hours on duty, but I did not know where or by whom. I forgot to ask when I got the assignment. So I continued my hiking. It was almost the same as my typical liberties on shore where I would hike all around the town and the adjacent areas.

The rest of the afternoon, and into the evening, I hiked on the sidewalks, went into the bars to be sure there was nothing unruly going on, and admired the scenery.

Early in the evening, as I was dutifully walking my beat, a pretty young French girl came to me, walked alongside me, and spoke to me in English. She told me that her name is France Manca. She walked along with me for several hours and we became rather well acquainted. Then she met up with her sister and they began their walk to their home. However, before she left, she invited me to come to her home and meet her parents tomorrow evening. I agreed to meet her down town the next day and I would walk with her and her sister to their home to meet her parents.

I was still walking my beat on the sidewalks of Oran when midnight arrived, so I went back to the ship, having completed a 16 hour beat as a shore-patrolman.

Jack, dressed for shore patrol duty

The next day, because there were the two sisters, I asked my friend Bill Scharninghausen to go with me to meet the parents. We met the girls downtown and began our hike. They lived in the French quarter of the city, and to get there, we had to walk through the Arab Quarter and the Spanish Quarter. As we walked through the Arab quarter, the natives glared at us, then going through the Spanish quarter, the natives also glared at us. But there was no encounter of any kind. Finally we got to their home, went in the house. It was a beautiful house with fine furniture. The parents were nice people, very friendly people and spoke fairly good English. They served us each a jigger of some kind of an alcoholic drink. I was not a drinking person so I had no idea what it was, but I sipped it and drank it. It was a pleasant evening. We visited and talked for several hours, then close to midnight, we left and began our hike back to the downtown area and to our ship.

France Manca, Jack, Claudie Manca

We left their house, turned right and began walking on the sidewalk toward the downtown. With memories of Alexandria Egypt, I was a little concerned about the upcoming Arabs and Spaniards. So I suggested to Scharninghausen that perhaps instead of walking on the sidewalk, we should walk in the middle of the street. On the sidewalk, there were many narrow, dark passageways which appeared to be going to never never land. I could visualize some big Arab reaching out from the darkness and dragging us down the alley. Scharninghausen agreed, so we went into the street. There was almost no traffic on the street, so we hiked past the Spanish Quarter, the Arab Quarter, and safely arrived downtown and to the dock where our ship was moored. We went aboard the ship and headed for our bunks.

A HIKE TO THE TOP OF THE ROCK OF GIBRALTAR.

In June 1947, the ship anchored at the Rock of Gibraltar. There was a very large gun at the top of the Rock, which I found interesting. On the ship, we had very powerful binoculars mounted on a stand on the deck near the bridge. So I proceeded to scan the side of Gibraltar through the binoculars. First I looked at the big gun at the top of the Rock. It was aimed at the Straight of Gibraltar, which was the entry into the Mediterranean Sea from the Atlantic Oceam. Then I scanned the sides of the Rock. Throughout the sides of the Rock, there were many carved tunnels in which there were guns pointing outward.

Later that day, I went on liberty into the town of Gibraltar, which is located at the base of the Rock. After walking around the town for a while, I hiked up the side of the Rock, on a path that led to Alameda Park. It was a nice park with many flowers and benches for the visitors.

I followed the path, which went continuously upward through the park, then continued beyond the park. Following the path, I was still travelling upward on the side of the Rock. I decided that I would walk all the way to the top of the Rock to get a good look at that big gun. However, when I got to within 100 feet of the top of the hill, I was confronted by a British soldier with a rifle. He told me to halt and advised me not to go any closer to the top of the Rock. This seemed like a sincere and final warning, so I turned around and walked back down, through the park, and into the town below. I did not get a close look at the big gun. From Gibraltar, we began our cruise across the Atlantic and to the United States.

GOING BACK TO THE SHIP FROM A WEEKEND AT HOME, I GOT THERE LATE, AND MISSED THE SHIP. SHE WENT OUT TO SEA WITHOUT ME.

In October 1947, I was transferred from the USS Huntington to the USS Ellyson, a Destroyer, which operated out of the Newport Navy Base.

In November 1947, I was on a weekend liberty at home from the USS Ellyson. Whenever I went back to the ship from home, I always took a bus to New York City. From there I took a train to Providence Rhode Island. From Providence, I rode a bus to Newport. So, on Sunday evening, I left home on a bus headed for New York City. I napped on the bus. I knew that was not a problem because I got off the bus at its last stop, in New York City. However, at a stop in Newark, New Jersey, the man sitting in the seat next to me woke me up and said we are in Newark, is this where you want to get off? I thought he said New York, so I jumped out of my seat, grabbed my overnight bag, and got off the bus. When I got off the bus, I looked all around. Everything was dark. Even the station was dark and locked up, and I watched my bus go around the corner and take off.

Here I am, in Newark, New Jersey and everything is dark , and there is no life anywhere in sight. Fortunately, I did find a taxi. I told him my problem. He said he would drive me to the railroad station in New York City for fifteen dollars. That was a fair price for a rather long drive, however, it was a lot of money for a person who was getting paid $50.00 a month. I had no choice, I took him up on his offer.

After a rather long trip, we arrived at the railroad station. I missed the train that I normally take to Providence, so I waited an hour for the next one. As a result, I got back to the liberty boat dock around eight o'clock, but the last liberty boat to go back to the ship was at seven-thirty. But good fortune was with me. The Master-at-arms in charge of the liberty boats was there, and he told me that the last liberty boat did not make the trip because the water was too rough in the Bay. There were other people there that were there on time for the last boat, but since it did not run, they were considered to have returned on time. The Master-at –arms said he will say that I was on time too. So I went into the Navy Base, found a place to sleep and spent the night there. In the morning, as I was standing there looking out toward the bay, I watched my ship leaving the bay and heading out to sea. So as a result, I spent three days on the Base until my ship came back and anchored in the Bay. I then rode a liberty boat out to the ship. Believe it or not, I didn't even get into any trouble and all was well.

TAKING A HIKE IN THE JUNGLES OF TRINIDAD.

In January 1948, I was transferred to the USS Orion, a submarine tender, which was located in Balboa in the Panama Canal Zone.

To travel to Panama, I became a passenger on the USS President Adams, a troop transport ship. On the transport ship, I met, and became friends with Bob Filkins, another passenger assigned to the Orion. On the trip to Panama, the ship stopped in Trinidad. Filkens and I went on liberty to the town of Port of Spain. We walked around the town for a while, then we chose to go out into the countryside.

As we were walking along a country road, we saw a trail leading into a wooded area. We decided to follow that trail to see what was in that jungle. As we entered, I was very careful, so I was looking up into the trees to make sure that there was not a boa constrictor up there waiting to slither down onto us. We encountered no snakes, or other wildlife, while in the jungle.

So we returned to the road, and as we were walking out of the trail, we were encountered by a native of Trinidad. He did not know that we were coming out of the jungle and thought that we were just approaching it. He told us not to follow that path into the jungle, because several days before, a native of Trinidad went In there and was attacked by several wild boars, and dragged away never to be seen again. We thanked this person for his advice, went back to the road and stayed on the road.

PINEAPPLES, BOATING, SWIMMING, AND SUNSHINE ON THE RESORT ISLAND OF TABOGA.

Upon being settled as a crew member on the Orion, I frequently went into the town of Panama City. It was a fairly modern city with traffic in a disorganized manner going in all directions in the streets. After hiking all over the City in many times ashore, I heard about a resort island nearby where you could rent a little cabin and spend the weekend there. To get there, I was transported, for a fee, to the Island on a barge. I went there several times and found it relaxing and interesting. Then one weekend. Filkins and I both went to Taboga Island. We put on our swimming trunks in the morning and relaxed on the sandy beach, looking out into the sea.

While doing this, a young Tabogan boy offered to climb a tree and get each of us a pineapple for twenty-five cents each. We took him up on that offer. He skillfully climbed the tree and delivered a big, juicy, pineapple to each of us. I ate my entire pineapple in the manner that you would eat a watermelon. I broke the hard knobs off of the surface and bit into the soft interior.

Jack, 20 years old

After eating our pineapples, we were looking out to sea and saw a small island a short distance out in the sea. We decided that we would rent a rowboat and ride out to the island to see what was there. We took turns rowing the boat and kept going toward the island. After some time of hard rowing, we realized that the island did not seem to be getting any closer. We discussed the situation and decided that we will keep going.

Jack, 1948

Finally, after much time and much rowing, we arrived at the island. When we got there, we dragged our rowboat about twenty feet from the water's edge so that it would not float away.

The island was very small, had jutting rocks on it, and there was an old shack on the highest point of the island. There was nothing else. However, Filkins and I swam aound the island , the water was crystal clear, and we enjoyed our swim. After some time, we decided that we better start back for Taboga.

We went to the side of the island, where we first arrived, to get our rowboat. The boat was still where we left it, but it was now about fifty feet from the water's edge. We forgot about the tide. The tide went out and our boat was higher from the water than where we left it. Then it dawned on me. The change in height from low tide to high tide in the Panama area is about twenty feet. If the tide had come in instead of out, our boat would have floated away and we would have been stranded on our little island.

Filkins contemplating our return trip to Taboga

With that good thought in our minds, we dragged the boat back into the water, got in, and started to row. It was a long and difficult ride back to Taboga Island.

That sounds like the end of this story, but there is more. After going back to the ship, I laid in my bunk and got some sleep. When I woke in the morning, I was in agony with sunburn all over my body. In addition, my mouth was sore from the acid in the pineapple, and I had sandflea bites from laying on the sandy beach. For the next week, or a little more, the only clothes that I wore was my underwear to minimize my sunburn pain. Fortunately we were in port, so I could hide on the bridge because almost no one came up there while we were in port.

A VISIT TO THE RUINS OF OLD PANAMA CITY

I went to the ruins of old Panama City on many occasions. To get there from the new Panama City, I took a bus to its last stop on the outside of town. From there, I either hiked to the ruins of Old Panama City, or sometimes, I hiked to a horse stable nearby, rented a horse, and rode horseback into the old city

Old Panama city was attacked and burned by pirates in the 1600's.

On my first trip to the ruins, as I walked among the remains of buildings, I saw a llama standing nearby eating grass. So I walked over to the llama, reached up to pet him, and he immediately spit what looked like tobacco juice on the front of my white uniform. He was a nice llama, but I never tried to pet him again. The splatter covered quite an area on my uniform, however, it stayed there for the rest of the day, and for my trip back to the ship. On the ship, I took the jumper off and threw it into the laundry.

The horse that I rented for some of my trips into the Ruins of Old Panama was trained English style, so when I mounted the horse and tried to get him to go in the direction that I wanted, he just stood there, or backed up a little. Someone noticed my problem and explained to me how the horse was trained and what I should be doing to have him follow my instructions. With my new knowledge, the horse and I got along fine. So I left the stable area and headed for the ruins. The horse chose to walk slowly, which was ok to me. Then we came to a little ravine where I suggested to the horse that he should jump over it. However he just stood there. So I dismounted, took the reins, and led him across the ravine, then remounted. We made it successfully to the ruins, and spent some time there looking around. For the return trip, I proceeded to head toward the horse stables. The horse sensed where we were going. Apparently this made him happy because he took off in a gallop to go home. When we came to the ravine, without slowing down, he leaped across it and kept going. The horse and I got along reasonably well, so I always chose him whenever I was making the trip.

The USS Orion AS-18

Jack, at sea, steering the USS Orion

Bananas for lunch in Panama

THE USS ORION ANCHORED OFF SAN JOSE ISLAND IN THE PACIFIC OCEAN- THE CREW WENT SWIMMING

The crew on San Jose Beach

On June 13, 1948, while anchored near San Jose Island, those members of the crew of the USS Orion who wished to participate in a swimming excursion, were tranported by the ships's liberty boats to the beach at the uninhabited San Jose island where they went ashore and spent the afternoon on the beach and swimming.

The liberty boats took us to the Island. When the boats got to within 50 feet of the beach, we were told that the boat could get no closer, and the swimmers should swim into the beach from this location. So I jumped into the water, as all of the others did, and swam into the beach. After spending several hours on the beach, we went back to the ship.

The next day, the same procedure was carried out, and I went to the beach on a liberty boat along with many others. When we arrived at the beach, the liberty boat stopped 300 feet from the shore and we were told that this is as close as we can get. We were told that everyone should swim to the shore. Everyone jumped in the water, including me, and swam toward the beach. The problem with this was that I was not a good swimmer. I swam doggie paddle, and I was capable of swimming a distance of fifty feet. So, I swam the fifty feet, and I could not swim any further, however, it was either swim or drown. So I kept swimming. Other swimmers going past me could see that I was struggling, and advised me to keep going. So I kept doggie paddling and was slowly getting closer to the beach. Finally, very tired, I reached the beach, climbed inland and layed down to rest for about fifteen minutes.

There were others that had the same problem. After swimming or resting on the beach for several hours, the boat took us back to the ship

Drinking coconut milk with a straw

LISTENING TO MUSIC ON THE RADIO ON THE ORION

While serving on the USS Orion, when the ship was in port, which was most of the time, I spent my off- time in the evening in the chart house. It was somewhat isolated because it was off limits for most of the crew. But I, being a quartermaster, could be there any time I wanted to. In the chart house, I could write letters, or work on my photo album, or visit with friends. When alone in the chart house, I enjoyed listening to music on the radio. There was one drawback to listening to the radio. Hanging on the bulkead was a very big radio, but it had no speaker. The only way I could listen to it was to plug in a set of earphones and wear them the whole time I sat in there. I felt like I was on a leash.

One evening, I got a brilliant idea. In the charthouse, mounted on an adjacent bulkhead was a fathometer. A fathometer measures the depth of the water In the location of the ship. Upon command, it electrically transmits a beep down to the bottom of the ocean. The beep echos off of the bottom and bounces back to the fathometer. In so doing, it has measured the depth of the water. The beeps are audible to the operator through a speaker in the fathometer.

My brilliant idea was to , somehow, connect the radio to the fathometer speaker. I attempted to find some existing terminals on the radio that I could work with to make that connection. There was a narrow space between the back of the radio and the adjacent bulkhead. I reached with my hand into the space to find something that I could connect to. I made a connection to something electrical back there with my hand, but it shocked me and sent me spinning across the chart house. I gave up on that idea.

Then I thought of another possibility. I picked up the earphones that are normally plugged into the radio. I cut the earphones off of the plug and wire. Then I plugged the earphone plug into the radio. I spliced wires onto the two wires coming from the plug, ran the wires unnoticeably along the bulkhead to the fathometer. I then connected them to the fathometer speaker. Now I was ready to see if it worked. I turned on the radio, and to my joy, music came from the fathometer. From that time onward, when I wanted to listen to the radio, I would plug my wire into the radio and listen to that good Panamanian music coming rom the speaker in the fathometer.

Jack 1948

AN AIRPLANE FLIGHT TO COSTA RICA

On September 5, 1948, an 18 year old kid named Tremblay, and I left the ship and went into Panama City on liberty. In spite of his age, Tremblay was a licensed pilot, at least he told me that he was. So Tremblay and I went to the local airport in Panama City and rented a plane, a Cessna 120. We decided to fly to Santa Clara Beach in Costa Rica to go swimming. We took off from the airport and headed north. After flying for a while, Tremblay pointed out a very dark cloud that filled half of the sky up ahead of us. He said that perhaps we should turn around and go back to Panama. I looked at the cloud and said why don't we just bear to the right and fly around the cloud. Of couse I had no idea what I was talking about. However, Tremblay said yes we could probably do that and he turned the plane and proceeded to try to fly around the storm cloud.

Amazingly enough, we did fly around the cloud and found clear weather on the other side. We continued to fly until we were apparently in the area of our destination. However, Tremblay looked at our chart. Then he looked at the ground and said that he can't find the airport. Circling around a little more, he concluded that a grassy area below with tire tracks was probably the airport, so we approached the area and he began his approach for a landing. When we were almost down for the landing, say about 50 feet off the ground, a cow walked out in front of us. Tremblay hit the gas and pulled the plane upward to miss the cow. We then circled the field and tried again. This time we successfully landed and it turned out that we really were on the airport.

We put our swimming trunks on and went to the beach. After several hours there, we got back in the plane and flew back to Panama.

Jack, 1949

A DUMB IDEA THAT WAS SCWELCHED BEFORE IT HAPPENED

While serving on the USS Orion, just as they do on all of the ships of the American fleet, when anchored or moored to a dock, there is always a watch on the quarterdeck where the gangway to the dock exists. This watch is made up of an Officer of the Deck, who is in charge of the watch detail, and a Quartermaster, a Messenger, and at times a Boatswains Mate. During the daytime, there is more activity on the ship, and each person is usually busy performing his duties.

However, on the mid-watch, from midnight until four in the morning, it is usually quiet on the quarterdeck. One such quiet night, as we usually did on quiet nights, we were making conversation among those present. I was the quartermaster of the watch, and Chief Warrant Boatswain McCarty was the officer of the deck. McCarty was a good man, a good officer and always willing to discuss things. As part of our conversation, I mentioned to McCarty that on this coming Saturday, when I will have a day of liberty from the ship, I am thinking about taking a walk down to the nearby swamps to look over the area, and possibly find, and observe, some alligators. McCarty's answer was, "can you run 21 miles per hour?" My answer to this was, "no I can't." Then he told me that alligators can run 20 miles per hour. In thinking about this, I determined that I probably should not hike down to the swamps. Looking back on this, at that time I knew nothing about alligators. Today, I know that they lurk near the edge of the water, in the weeds, and when some hapless prey walks by, they leap out and take a big bite onto the preys legs, then proceeds to eat it.

Although I usually ignored advice, It was good that I followed the good advice of McCarty. Boatswain McCarty probably saved my life.

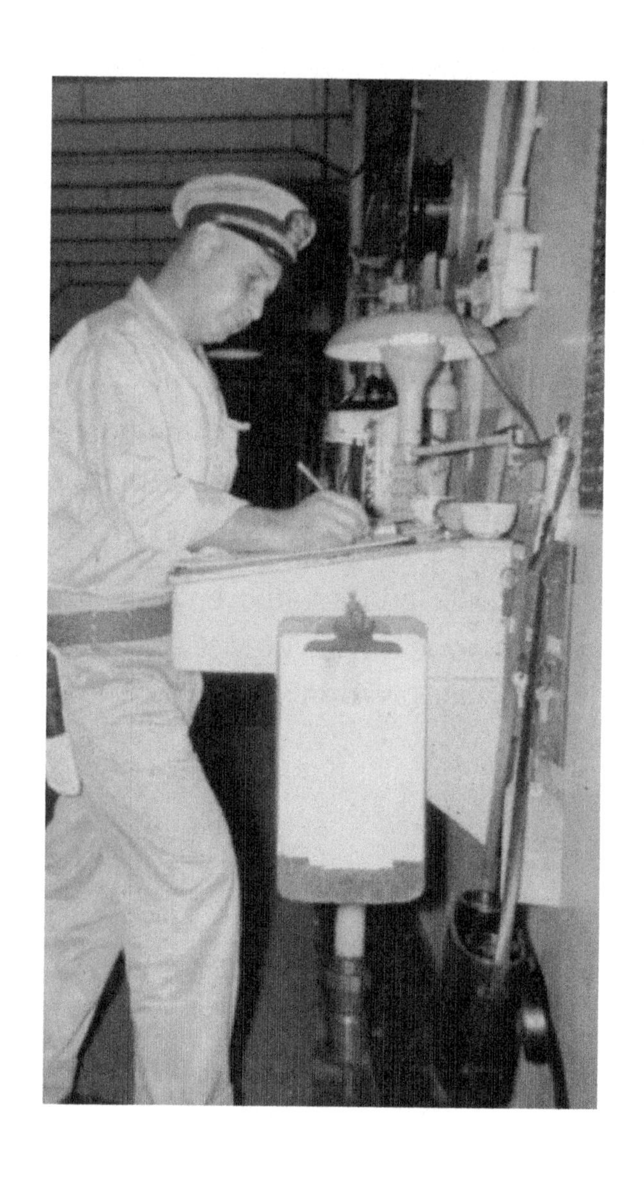

Chief Warrant Boatswain McCarty

PLAYED A GAME OF GOLF

On September 28, 1948, along with several other members of the Orion's crew, I went to the Naval Ammunition depot golf course. I never played golf before, but the equipment was provided to us when we checked in. However, I received no instructions on the fine procedures of golfing. We took turns placing our ball on a tee at the beginning point then whacked it with the club. The others did not play the game much better than I did. It took us quite a long time to play through nine holes. At that time we concluded that we had enough. I justified stopping at that point because our scores were high enough that it appeared that we played the entire course.

There was one little incident, in which I was involved, during my day on that golf course. At the one hole, the tee- off point was on a hill, then it sloped down into a low area, and the next hole was also on a hill. As I was ready to tee off, two marines approached from the side and started walking in front of me in the low area. I figured that they were way down there and when I whack the ball it will whiz by far above their heads, so I whacked the ball and it whizzed by them well above their heads. However, the marines took issue and screamed at me for not yelling “fore”. I figured if they were stupid enough to walk in front of me when I was teeing off, its their problem, not mine.

IN MARCH 1949, I WAS HONORABLY DISCHARGED FROM THE NAVY. I WENT TO COLLEGE, GRADUATED, AND GOT A JOB WITH AN ENGINEERING FIRM, THEN DROVE MY CAR OVER A CLIFF.

Having completed my four year enlistment in the Navy, I was now back home and was a civilian. I got a job working for a friend of my Dad, Mr. Oscar Dockey. I was employed to maintain his lawns, flowers, and garden, and to plant trees, plus any other work that Mrs. Dockey may have decreed. Mr. Dockey was the Superintendent of a cemetery and he was also a stone mason by trade. He built his stone house out of discarded tombstones.

I worked for Mr. Dockey all summer, then in September of 1949, I left to go to college in Fort Wayne, Indiana. I attended college year round and graduated in June of 1952 with the degree, Bachelor of Science in Civil Engineering.

PRELIMINARY SITE WORK FOR THE DESIGN AND CONSTRUCTION OF A FLOOD CONTROL DAM

Jack, 1951

Upon graduation, I returned to Pennsylvania and went to work for an Engineering Firm in Harrisburg, Pennsylvania.

My first assignment with the engineering firm was to go to the site of a proposed flood control dam to be constructed on a small tributary of the Susquehanna River in Cameron County, Pennsylvania.

I was to take command of the entire operation which would include all property surveys necessary to acquire the land that will be flooded by the dam, and to conduct all surveys necessary for the design of the dam embankment. The work would also include the supervision of physical drilling operations to determine the types of soil involved, and any bedrock.

We established an office in an old farmhouse near the site of the proposed dam. This farmhouse would also become the temporary home for the primary people to be hired to oversee the various phases of the work.

Four qualified instrument men were hired to lead the proposed survey crews. The other personnel necessary to form the survey crews would be hired from the local area, and would be trained to do the work. We referred to them as Mountain Men.

An office manager type was hired to organize and control the necessary research and paper shuffling that would be necessary. The office manager's name was Jack Franklin. A drilling company was hired to provide the operators, and the equipment, to do the investigative drilling.

The office manager and I quickly became good friends. The only town within range of our office and working place was the town of Emporium.

We went there amost every evening just to be around other people.

DIGGING A HOLE TO GET A SAMPLE OF THE SOIL FOR TESTING PURPOSES.

On one occasion, the home office of the company, in Harrisburg, Pennsylvania, instructed me to have someone dig a hole about four feet deep in the area where they anticipated that we would remove soil to be used for the fill of the embankment of the dam. We were then instructed to bag a sample of the soil and have it sent to our office in Harrisburg.

Rather than assigning the project of aquiring the sample of soil to someone else, Franklin and I decided to do it ourselves. We loaded our truck with digging equipment and drove to the site to dig the hole. Upon arriving there, we found a location in the shade where we would dig the hole. Franklin used the pick, and I used the shovel. After a few minutes of hard work, we both agreed that digging this hole is very difficult.

Franklin came up with a brilliant idea. He suggested that we go to a supply house, several miles away, where drillers drilling for natural gas In the area went to buy their supplies. So we went to the supply house and bought a bag full of dynamite sticks along with quite a few feet of fuse.

Going back to our work site, we went to the shallow hole that we dug and pushed several sticks of dynamite into the hole. Then we connected the fuse and stretched it out over about fifteen feet. We lit the fuse then ran back some distance and we each hid behind a tree.

We waited and waited some more. The fire on the fuse was moving very slowly. Finally after a long wait, the dynamite blew. Rocks and dirt flew into the air. We came out of our hiding places and ran over to see what we accomplished. The hole got a little bigger and a little deeper, but not deep enough. We, therefore, began the process of reloading the hole again with dynamite, using a few more sticks than we did for the initial blast.

This time we used a somewhat shorter fuse, lit the fuse, went to our hiding places and waited for the blast. This blast threw more dirt, and much higher, than the first blast, so when everything settled down, we returned to the hole. The center of the hole was a little over three feet deep, so we cleaned the hole out, and with our pick and shovel, we dug into the bottom of the hole and retrieved enough soil to fill our canvas bag. We took the bag to the local Greyhound Bus station and paid the driver to take it with him to Harrisburg where our bosses could pick it up.

TRANSPORTING A SURVEY CREW ACROSS THE FIRST FORK CREEK.

On one occasion, one of our survey crews wanted to survey on the opposite side of the First Fork Creek, but they did not know how to get there. It was early in the morning and it had rained most of the night. The water in the creek was flowing at a quite rapid velocity, and the water was much deeper than usual. Furthermore, there was no road or bridge across the creek in that area.

I knew where there was a location in the stream in that area where locals forded the stream with their trucks, so I told the crew that I will drive them across the stream with my company panel truck. I loaded the survey crew and all of their equipment into the panel truck. The stream at the time was about 50 feet wide.

We then approached the edge of the stream, drove into it, and headed for the other side. The water from the stream started to trickle into the cab of the truck around the edges of the doors. We kept moving and bouncing over many rocks in the streambed. I was aiming for a certain cut in the stream bank on the other side of the stream. I had the truck in low gear and kept feeding gas, but we moved rather slowly, and at the same time we were not only crossing the stream, but we were also drifting somewhat sideways and downstream. The members of the survey crew were sitting in the back of the truck, and cheering me on. Finally, we reached the opposite side of the stream, but we were about fifteen feet further downstream from the destination that I had in mind. So I gave the truck more gas and drove up a fairly steep bank on the other side of the stream and successfully reached the opposite side with the survey crew.

The survey crew got out of the truck, set up their equipment, and proceeded to do their surveying. Since the stream was so wild, I decided to stay there with the crew until they completed their work, then I would drive tham back across the creek. I have to admit that I kept watching the stream and thinking that going back across could be a problem. Finally, after several hours of surveying, the crew was ready to return to the other side of the creek. So we loaded all the equipment, and all of the survey crew, and drove over the bank into the stream, fed the gas, bounced on the rocks, and successfully crossed back to the other side.

We then drove back to our field office.

DRIVING TO INDIANA TO VISIT FRIENDS, THEN DROVE BACK TO OUR FIELD OFFICE.

Getting back to when I was in college in Indiana, I became friends with a waitress in my favorite restaurant. This friendship developed even more up to the point where I was invited to her home and met the rest of the family. Her parents, brothers, and younger sister were also great people. I visited them regularly, and over a period of time, this developed into a situation where I was accepted into the family. This relationship grew over the years, and eventually I was considered as a member of the family.

Therefore, while living and working in Pennylvania, I quite regularly took off on a Friday evening and drove the 500 miles to their Indiana farm to visit. While working on the flood control dam project, I made this trip usually every two weeks. I would stay with my adopted family over the weekend, then on Sunday evening I would leave the farm and begin my journey back to Pennsylvania. It took about ten hours to drive from my workplace to the farm in Indiana.

On one of my trips out there, I did not leave the farm until close to ten o'clock at night. I was supposed to be back to my office by 8:00 the next morning. Usually on these trips I didn't have any trouble staying awake. However, this tme, I did ok driving out of Indiana, and across Ohio, but when I entered western Pennsylvania and got to within fifty miles of my destination, I began to get a little sleepy. The road that I was on was a winding mountain road with very little traffic, and with very little population. There was no place to stop for coffee. It got to the point that periodically, I would stop the car, walk around it, get back in the car, slap my face and move on. Finally, although I was very sleepy, I only had about ten more miles to go and I would be back to the office. So I kept going. The road wound along this desolate area, containing many curves and hugging the side of a mountain. On one side of the road, the land sloped downward about 1000 feet. Finally, I came to an area where the road curved to the right, there was a ravine on the left side of the road where it sloped downward at least 100 feet, and on the right side was the 1000 foot drop. As I approached that curve, apparently I fell asleep, I was probably moving at a speed of about fifty miles per hour. As I went more into sleep, my foot pressed down on the gas pedal. Then there was a loud noise where the car smashed through a guard rail fence and knocked out several posts which were supporting it. The car went airborne into the ravine, taking limbs off the tops of the trees as it sailed by. I woke up and saw the green branches flying by as I passed through the tops of the trees. I remember thinking that this is not a good thing. Then I came to a smashing stop as I hit the ground and ran into a rock formation which stopped the car. I got out of the car on the low side, for the car was setting on sloped ground and leaning downhill. I never gave it a thought that the car may roll down the hill and in so doing, roll over me. After I got out of the car, I noticed that the headlights were still on, so I opened the door and turned out the lights, then slammed the door shut again. Once again I walked away from the car, but then I saw a mutilated hubcap laying on the ground, so I picked it up, again opened the door and threw the hubcap inside and slammed the door shut. Finally, I walked toward the road, which was up an embankment about fifty feet above me. I climbed the embankment and reached the shoulder of the road. I then began walking along the shoulder until I stepped into a hole, with both legs, which I created by knocking the guard rail posts out. With my legs in the hole on the shoulder of the road, I laid back and fell asleep.

I don't know how long I was sleeping there, until a man who was driving by stopped, woke me up, and was trying to talk to me. He asked me if I was hurt, and my answer was I don't know. He asked if there is anyone else in the car, and my answer was I don't know. He probably went down to the car to check while I slept.

When I again awoke, there were two men standing there talking to me. They wanted to find out which way I was going so they could give me a ride to somewhere. I had friends in the little village of Driftwood, which was about five miles up the road. The friends were two guys that worked on the drills at the dam site. The second man to arrive, of the two men, was going in that direction, so they led me to his car. I got in the car, and the first man said to the second man that he should keep an eye on me when I get out of the car because "he is badly dazed".

We arrived in Driftwood and I pointed out the friend's house. The driver stopped the car, I got out, walked across some railroad tracks and onto the porch of the house. I knocked on the door. One of the two men opened the door and was surprised to see me. He invited me in, and as I walked across their living room floor, blood was dripping from my leg. They noticed that all was not well with me, so after I explained the circumstances to them as well as I could, they loaded me in their car and drove me to our field office at the dam site.

Realizing that I did not look too good, our office manager loaded me into his car and drove me to a hospital in the town of Coudersport. They sat me on a table while a nurse questioned me. When she asked what happened, I told her that I drove my car over a cliff. She asked me who I worked for and what I did. I told her that I was a dam engineer.

This conversation did not last very long. Although I did bump my head, my only real injuries were my knees. They were both cut because of the impact of hitting the rock on the hillside and coming to an instant stop which sent my knees crashing into the dashboard. They bandaged my knees and told me I could go back to work.

A WEEKEND DRIVE TO INDIANA AND BACK

In connection with this, prior to working on the Flood control dam site, and before I drove my plymouth over the cliff, when I first went to work for the Engineering firm in Harrisburg, I also made regular weekend runs to the farm in Indiana. From Harrisburg, I took the Pennsylvania turnpike to the Ohio Line. At that point, the Ohio turnpike did not yet exist, so I took Route 30 through Ohio, and into Indiana. Without the Ohio turnpike, it took twelve hours to get to the farm. In making that trip, I usually never got out of the car. At the Ohio line, I always needed gas, so I would stop for gas. In those days the attendent at the gas station would pump the gas for the customer. I would sit in the car while he did this, then I would pay him and take off for Indiana.

On one of those trips back to Pennsyvania, the roads all the way, had a slick coat of frozen rain on the road. There was very little traffic on the road, and I was driving cautiously at twenty five miles per hour, so this trip took a little longer than usual.

Eventually, I arrived at the Allegheny tunnel on the Pennsylvania turnpike, which is close to the top of a mountain, so when I exited the eastern end of the tunnel, there was a very steep portion of the highway leading downward from the tunnel. In addition, the sloped highway was also very icy. When I arrived at the exit to the tunnel, there was a tractor trailer parked there. He told me that he was waiting for a highway cinder truck to come along and cinder the hill, then he will go ahead. I told him that I guess I will try going down the hill. So I started down the hill, but foolishly at too great a speed. I no sooner started down the hill when I went into a spin, rotating and making circles on the highway as I was going uncontrolled down the hill. Luckily, in my rotating process, I spun off the right side of the road and ran into a cinder pile. The cinder pile stopped me without any damage to the car. I backed out of the cinder pile, got back onto the highway, put the car in low gear, and kept two wheels on the shoulder of the road where there was less ice. By this method, I drove slowly down the hill, slid no more, and finally reached the bottom of the hill and continued on my way. I arrived in Harrisburg, and all was well.

THE 1928 MODEL A FORD

My 1949 plymouth was totalled as a result of my driving it over a cliff, so on my next trip to Indiana, I travelled by bus. While in Indiana, the father of the Indiana group took me into Fort Wayne. There we went to a used car lot and I purchased, for $100, a 1928 model A ford pickup truck. Although it was not in perfect shape, I drove it back to the farm.

The 1928 Model A Ford

For transportation back to Pennsylvania, I chose to drive my new truck. The top logical speed for the truck was about 35 miles per hour. Even then, the engine was racing because the truck was supposed to have 19- inch wheels on it but the previous owner replaced them with 15-inch wheels. Therefore the engine had to work harder than it should.

Apparently, because the engine was being overworked, as I was proceeding through eastern Ohio, one of the pistons in the engine broke and rattled with a loud noise. However, the truck kept running, so I kept going. Soon, as I was rattling along, it began to get dark. I tried to turn the headlights on, but they did not work. I could still see the road, so I kept going. It got darker, but it happened to be a night with a full moon, so I could still see the road. After driving for about thirty miles, I crossed the border into Pennsylvania with no headlights and the engine making loud cracking noises. As I entered a small town, a local policeman stopped me. He said that I was driving without headlights to which I innocently responded that , yes, they just went out, I don't know what happened. So I opened the hood while the policeman held a flashlight so that I could try to figure out what was wrong and, therefore fix it. I had no idea of how to make the lights work. There were wires dangling everywhere. The policeman suggested that I should pull over and park the truck and wait until daylight to proceed. I told him that I would do that. After the policeman left, I cranked the truck to try to get it started, but it would not start. Two drunks came along and wanted to crank the truck, so I gave one of them the crank. He tried, but he could not start the truck. He got angry and threw the crank down the middle of the street, then the two of them left. I then walked down the street and retrieved my crank. About that time, it was about midnight, two truckers came out of a restaurant across the street. I asked them if they would push my truck across the street so that I could drift down an alley that sloped slightly downhill, and hopefully, I could start the engine on compression. They pushed the truck across the street, and as it moved down the alley, I tried to start it. When I did that, it let out a loud backfire and the two truckers immediately walked away. However, the truck still continued to go down the alley, and the engine started. Now, with the noisy engine running, in the alley it was very dark and I could see nothing. Luckily, two men were walking nearby, so I asked for directions. They told me to turn right and go up another alley a short distance, then turn right again into another alley which will take me out to the main street. I thanked them and proceeded to do what they told me. As I was driving along in the second alley, I was looking to the right trying to locate the alley that would take me out to the main street. I finally found a clearing, that, in the dark, appeared to be an alley. So I turned right and drove clatteringly between two houses, which turned out to be someone's back yard, then proceeded to the main street, where I dropped off of a curbline, and turned left on the main road. Once on the main road, I was going east headed for home. Of course, I still didn't have any headlights. On the outskirts of town, I came to a steep hill that sloped downward. I concluded that this would be a good place to spend the rest of the night because , In the morning I could drift down the hill and start the engine on compression. So I pulled over to the edge of the road, turned off the engine, and layed down on the seat to sleep. However, I could not stretch out because the seat of the truck was not wide enough.

To solve that problem, I opened the truck's window, hung my legs out the window resting the knees on the bottom of the window opening. I slept well, and in the morning when it got daylight, I drifted the truck down the hill and started the engine, and once again I was on my noisy way to the field office and my home.

Without any further problems, in a few hours, I arrived at the field office ready for work.

COMPLETED WORK ON THE FLOOD CONTROL DAM. AND RETURNED TO OUR HARRISBURG OFFICE.

I was at my parent's home in Camp Hill, Pennsylvania, when My Dad, my brother, Bill, and I decided to drive up to the site of the flood control dam near Emporium to bring back my model A Ford which was still up there.

We went up in my 1952 Buick. When we got there, I got in the model A ford, started it ,and drove it to Camp Hill. Bill and Dad followed me in the 1952 Buick.

For quite some time, the model A was parked on the street in front of my parents house. My Mother was not too happy with that ugly thing setting out there, so I agreed to remove it.

I did not know what to do with it, so my Dad suggested that we take it down to his sister's farm in southern York County and give it to them. That seemed like a good solution, so in preparation to do that, I backed my Buick up against the front bumper of the Model A. Then with a bunch of rope, I tied the two bumpers together. I put the Model A in neutral.

Dad and I got into my car, and I drove away from the curb, bringing the model A along. Our destination was at least 50 miles away. We drove southward on the highway, then eventually we drove through the City of York. Going around some of the curves at the urban intersections, I had to swing it wide because the rope connection between the two cars was quite rigid. Eventually, we arrived at the farm. At my Uncle's suggestion, we parked the model A in the middle of a grassy field on the farm. My uncle was now the owner of the Model A.

HIKING IN A MUDDY DITCH DURING THE REPAIRS TO THE LITTLE PINE CREEK DAM.

Upon the completion of the surveying and other initial work for the proposed flood control dam on the First Fork creek, I was sent to the site of the Little Pine Creek Flood Control Dam, an existing dam near Jersey Shore, PA, as the Resident Engineer for repairs to be made to the dam to correct some deficiencies.

One day, while observing some work in progress, I was wading in shallow water wearing my boots. I was watching a backhoe excavating a trench along the edge of the waterway in which large rocks would be placed to stabilize the edge. After watching the trench being excavated, I decided to leave that part of the project and go to another area. So I walked to the edge of the stream to climb a bank to move on to the other area. When I arrived at the edge of the stream, I stepped into the trench which I had just watched them dig, landing on the bottom of the trench into muddy water above my waist. I don't believe that the backhoe operator was impressed with my engineering abilities.

A STEEP HILL WITH A U-CURVE AT THE BOTTOM

In 1955, while working for the engineering firm in their Harrisburg office, I designed a dam for a girl scout camp near Berwick, PA.

The dam was nearing completion, so I drove up to the dam site and observed the dam and talked to the contractor.

Upon completion of this errand, I left the site driving a company car, and headed back to the Harrisburg office. It was getting late in the day and I would not get back to the office until after office closing time. So I decided to take a slight detour in my return trip to visit my Uncle and Aunt in Bear Gap, PA. I arrived at their house and visited with them for quite a while, then I left and continued my return trip to Harrisburg.

As I was approaching the village of Gowen City, I was cruising along at an approximate speed of 50 miles per hour. It was raining with a fine drizzle at the time. I was thinking, or possibly day dreaming, and was not really paying attention to my driving when I suddenly realized that I was traveling down a steep hill and there was a u-turn near the bottom of the hill. I hit the brakes, but because the road was wet, the car just bounced a little but did not appreciably slow down. As I got closer to the curve, I realized that I only had about three options. I could try going around the curve at an unsafe speed, but the car would probably roll over, or I could go straight instead of going around the curve, but I would smash into trees, so I concluded that I would swing the car very wide as I approached the curve and try to scrape the adacent bank with the front bumper of the car, and hopefully this would slow me down enough to safely make it around the curve. So, I was driving on the wrong side of the road and scraping the adjacent bank with the bumper as I approached the curve. Suddenly, the bumper must have snagged something in the bank because the car suddenly spun around and faced up the hill and came to a stop. I drifted the car backwards toward the curve and backed off the paved road on to a wide area adjacent to the road and stopped the car. The engine had stopped, the car stopped and I sat there for a little while. Then I started the engine, turned the car around, and resumed my drive toward Harrisburg. As I passed through the village of Gowen City, I stopped the car under a street light, got out of the car, and looked it over thoroughly. As far as I could see, there was no damage to the car. I drove to Harrisburg.

BEING LOYAL TO A FRIEND, I PROBABLY DID SOMETHING DUMB.

In 1955, while working in the Harrisburg office of the engineering firm, an old friend came to visit me at my parents house in Camp Hill, PA. You may remember reading earlier in this book about the preliminary work for the design of a flood control dam in Cameron County, where Jack Franklin and I met and became friends. Well, Jack Franklin was the friend who came to visit me in Camp Hill.

I had not seen him since we worked together several years before, and, of course, I was very glad to see him. He visited with me and my parents throughout the evening. We invited him to stay overnight at our house and he accepted that invitation.

My parents retired to bed sometime around 11:00 o'clock, then, as was our custom in our earlier days together, Franklin and I decided to go to a diner in Harrisburg to enjoy a steak.

We took my car, and, of course, I drove to the diner, parked my car on the street, and we went into the diner, sat in a booth and both of us ordered a very large steak. While we were eating our steaks, two Harrisburg policemen came into the diner and sat at the counter. After about a half hour, we had finished our steaks and were ready to leave the diner and return to my parents' home.

We paid for our food and headed for the door of the diner. We noticed that the two policemen were still sitting at the counter. I did not mention this earlier, but Franklin liked his alcoholic beverages and I was a tee- totaler. Franklin was a little on the teetering side as we exited the diner.

When we got outside onto the sidewalk, there was a police car parked along the curb with its engine running. Franklin, in his inebriated manner irately proclaimed that it was illegal to park the car, unattended, along the curb with the engine running. So he got into the car, backed it up about fifty feet, then backed it into an alley. I waited, in front of the diner, for him to return. After a few minutes he emerged from the alley with a big smile on his face while tossing the car keys into the air and catching them. I confronted him and told him that he could have at least left the keys in the car. He smiled and said OK. He returned to the car to leave the keys. When he again arrived at the front of the diner, I asked him if he put the keys into the car and he said he did. He opened the car door and threw the keys inside.

The policemen were still in the diner. Here I was, an unwilling partner in a rather serious situation, so I concluded that the best thing to do is to load Franklin into my car and get out of there. We got into the car and returned to my parents' home.

I suppose the proper thing to do in that situation would have been to lead Franklin, and the keys to the car, into the diner and apologize to the policemen. I am sure that would have led to a lot of trouble.

For the next several days, I expected that a policeman would be knocking on our door. Surely someone witnessed the event and would give the information to the police, but it never happened.

I protected my wayward friend, but could have been involved in a very embarassing siuation.

I GOT MARRIED AND WE WENT ON OUR HONEYMOON.

Several years after the projects with the construction of the dams, I was twenty-nine years old. I married a 19 year old young lady. (Yes, I am familiar with the title of this composition, but we will not get into that.) However, since she was nineteen and an orphan, she had no one to sign for her, so we could not get married in Pennsylvania. So we went to Towsen, Maryland and were married.

For our honeymoon, I chose to head South, of course not knowing what our final destination would be, we drove through Virginia. We drove westward, and on the skyline Drive. We eventually ended up in the western end of North Carolina. As we drove along, we found Chimney Rock, which looked interesting to us, so we went into the area and, parked the car. There was a sign there that said we could go inside the building and take an elevator to the top of the rock, or we could hike up a trail that wound around the rock. I made the choice that we should hike up the trail.

So we followed the narrow trail as it twisted around the rock. As we got further up the trail, the dropoff at the edge of the trail kept getting higher. I don't think my new wife was too impressed with my decision to walk up the trail, but she quietly hiked without any complaints. It so happens that we were doing this in January, and the weather was quite cold. So as we got higher on the trail, we were walking on sheets of ice on our narrow little trail. This required a little care in our foot placement so that we would remain on the trail. When we got near to the top of the Rock, we came to some wooden steps leading upward. However, the steps were covered with thick ice. I noticed that the formation of ice contained a tunnel near the bottom of the layer of ice. So we crawled through the tunnel under the ice and emerged at the top of the steps. We finally reached the top of Chimney Rock. The view from up there was fantastic. We could see long distances in all directions. After admiring the view for quite some time, I asked my wife if she wanted to hike back down on the trail, or did she want to go inside the adjoining building and go down in the elevator. She chose the elevator.

We Went down the elevator, left the building and got into our car to resume our travel. A short distance from chimney rock, we found some tourist cabins, so we decided to stop for the night. The facilities were closed because it was out of season for tourists, however, the lady that owned the cabins was so happy to see us that she rented one to us even though they were closed for the winter.

The next morning, we took off, headed west, and ended up in Asheville. It was an interesting town, so we walked around, went into the shops, and found a diner where we had dinner. We stayed in Asheville that night, then took off again going westward. I decided that we would like to cross over the Smokey Mountains into Tennessee, so we drove in that direction to find a road that crossed the mountain. However, when we got to the road over the mountain, we found that there were barricades placed across the road at the bottom of the mountain. I decided that there probably was no good reason for the barricades, so I got out of the car, moved the barricades out of the way, then drove my car past the barricades, then again got out of the car and replaced the barricades back into the location that they had been.

As we drove up the mountain, the scenery was great and we were going higher and higher. Before long, we were driving on ice, but the car had good traction so we continued upward. I had to be careful not to slide too much on the ice, because the dropoff at the edge was quite high. We made it up to the top of the mountain, then we started down the other side. Things were getting a little tricky. I wanted to go slowly, but when I used the brakes, I started sliding. I decided to put the car in low gear, that way I did not have to use the brakes as much. We crawled slowly down the icy hill, and managed to stay on the road, then we finally reached the bottom and we were in Tennessee. We drove through Tenessee, then headed North into Kentucky. We stayed overnight in Kentucky. When we got up in the morning, there was snow on the ground well over 12" in depth. I was driving my 1956 Buick, and it plowed through the deep snow quite well. We continued to drive through the snow all the way through Kentucky and again in West Virginia. We finally arrived at my parent's house in Pennsylvania, and our honeymoon trip had been completed. I am sure that my wife was happy with the choices that she made.

FEEDING MARSHMALLOWS TO A BLACK BEAR

In 1958, the engineering firm in Harrisburg that I was working for, sent me to Bradford, Pennsylvania to look after a project in progress in that town. So, my wife, Irmgard, and I, along with my nephew, Bill McSherry, drove to Bradford. We rented an apartment in a nice setting alongside the highway that went from Bradford into the state of New York. As usual, we travelled around to see what we could find. We drove on the highway, which passed by our apartment, and in about five miles of driving, we were in New York State. As soon as we crossed the border, we found the Allegheny State Park. It was a large, beautifull, and natural park. We watched the deer, the raccoons, and even some beavers building a dam on the edge of a lake.

We lived in that apartment for several months. The entire time that we were there, my nephew, Bill, stayed there with us. Bill was probably about seven years old at that time. We traveled all over the area and found many interesting things and sights. However, our favorite place was the Allegheny State Park. We enjoyed going there in the evening because that is when most of the animals were grazing in the fields alongside the road. We gave crackers to the raccoons, watched the deer, and occasionaly saw a bear.

On one occasion, I spotted a bear at the edge of the woods near the road, so I pulled the car over to the side of the road and parked. I wanted Irmgard and Bill to get a good look at the bear, so I got out of the car, carrying a small box of marshmallows. Irmgard and Bill stayed in the car. I opened the box, took out a marshmallow and threw it into the woods, toward the bear. The bear saw me do that, so he cautiously came closer. When he ate the first marshmallow, I threw some more to him, each one a little closer to the car. In a very short time, the bear was rather close to me as I kept feeding him marshmallows. However, as I was pulling the marshmallows from the box, I came to a cardboard divider between the layers of the marshmallows. That delayed me in getting the next marshmallow out of the box. By that time the bear came very close to me and stood on his hind legs right in front of me demanding another marshmallow. Standing on his hind legs, he must have been close to nine feet tall. So, I quickly, and urgently, pulled several more marshmallows out of the box, showed them to the bear and threw them about fifteen feet away. The bear left me to go to the marshmallows. I threw several more marshmallows as far as I could into the woods. I then got back into the car. Bill and Irmgard got a good look at the bear even though for a while they thought the bear was going to eat me.

PUT OUT A FIRE WITH A TOY FIRETRUCK

In 1964, our son, Jack III, at the age of four years, got a toy firetruck for Christmas. The firetruck had a water tank, a water pump, and a long hose with a nozzle. It was totally equipped to put out a fire. We, therefore, determined that we should make it work. We took the firetruck into our basement, placed some paper napkins and portions of newspaper on the concrete floor. Then we lit the paper with a match and created a nice big fire.

Jack III rushed to the fire with his firetruck and pumped water onto the burning paper. After pumping water onto the fire, though the hose, the fire was gradually put out.

Jack III was very happy with the great ability of his firetruck.

MY PET ROOSTER HAD SOME FUN

In the mid sixties, my daughter, Ellen, was about seven years old. At that time, I had a pet rooster, named Geronimo, who was several years old. Geronimo liked to fight with me, so I would put my foot out and he would jump on it, pecked my legs with his beak, and he clawed my leg with his spurs. He was enjoying himself beating me up, but then he would get tired. He began huffing and puffing. So I would pick him up, cradle him in my arms, and talked quietly to him. When he calmed down, I would put him down and let him go to do whatever he wanted to.

One day, as I was standing in the back yard, Ellen came running around the house at top speed, screaming and laughing. Then there came Geronimo, running at full speed about twenty feet behind her. Ellen circled the house again and went by me screaming for help. The rooster was about ten feet behind her. On the third circuit around the house, Ellen arrived, screaming for help, with the rooster about five feet behind her. I was enjoying the show, but the rooster was getting a little close, so I stepped in, picked up the rooster, petted him, and told him that he is a good rooster. Ellen was tired, but happy.

BUILDING A NEW FLOOR IN MY SON'S BARN.

Several years ago, I was helping my son, Patrick, build a new floor in his barn. The new floor system consisted of timber plank flooring supported by timber beams, and the timber beams being supported with timber columns.

We had temporary columns under the beams until we poured the concrete footings so that we could put in the final columns. We reached the point where the finished columns were in place. Since the final columns were all in their proper places, it was time to remove the temporary columns.

So I proceeded to lean my ladder against one of the temporary columns that was to be removed. I then climbed up the ladder and unattached the temporary column from the beam. Upon doing this, the temporary column fell over, my ladder fell over, and I jumped from the ladder and landed safely and upright on the dirt floor below.

Patrick suggested to me that perhaps he should remove the remaining temporary columns himself.

Jack and Friend

Oh well, I guess that's the way it goes.

But, you should know, when I was discharged from the Navy, I received my

Good Conduct Medal.

Made in the USA
Middletown, DE
30 June 2020